Library of Congress catalog card number: 95-069544

ISBN number: 1-882792-14-9

Proctor Publication, LLC of Ann Arbor, Michigan, USA
PRINTED IN THE UNITED STATES OF AMERICA

PSALM 23

The Lord is My Sheperd; I shall not want.
He maketh me to lie down in green pastures:
He restoreth my soul; He leadeth me in the paths of
    righteousness for His name's sake.
Yea, though I walk through the valley of the shadow of death, I
    will fear no evil; for Thou art with me; Thy rod and Thy
    staff, they comfort me.
Thou preparest a table before me in the presence of mine
    enemies; Thou annointest my head with oil; my cup
    runneth over.
Surely goodness and mercy shall follow me all the days of my
    life; and I will dwell in the house of the Lord forever.

May I take a moment of your time
To say THANKS for reading a few lines,
Which God has given to share with you.
May you know His peace and love so true.

You might ask why I choose this title for my book. Everything I have written, God has given me. In the midnight hours, while the world sleeps, "GOD STILL SPEAKS IN THE MIDNIGHT HOURS." I pray it will be a blessing to your heart.

From

"GOD THROUGH MY HEART TO YOURS"

Velma Price Brookshire

CONTENTS

God Still Speaks In The Midnight Hours

By Velma Price Brookshire

I dedicate
God Still Speaks In The Midnight Hours
to my children,
Terry W. Quillen and
Glenda (Quillen) Enriquez,
and to my husband,
James F. Brookshire.

My heartfelt thanks to my husband for his support and patience with me when I stayed up all night pecking away on the typewriter; to our daughter-in-law, Jeannie Brookshire, for typing the poems onto a computer disk. A very special thanks and appreciation to Hazel Proctor, for putting the entire book together for me — I couldn't have done it without her.

The Dawning Of A New Day

What beauty and bliss watching the dawning of a new day,
Seeing the dew brightly glisten in the sun rays.
Hearing the birds sing their beautiful songs,
The darkness slowly fades away before very long.

It's a new day the moon and stars have gone out of sight,
The sun is peeping up now to show it's bright light.
LOOK! God's beauty to behold in the clouds of pretty pink,
Blue sky of Heaven, made without paint or ink.

In the stillness of the early dawn,
Sometimes a little fog will linger on.
Soon a tree top or two will come into view,
I pause and give Thanks, God unto You.

Thank You God, for another beautiful day,
For eyes to see all the wonders you have made.
And pray when the day has come to an end,
You will keep me until a new dawn begins.

Early dawn a wonderful time for Jesus to return,
I watch for you daily, and dearly yearn.
At Early Dawn as I gaze into the eastern sky,
I know my JESUS IS COMING in the sweet by and by.

Whispers Of Jesus

Jesus whispered to me in my early years
When I heard Him whisper so sweetly in my ears
Your soul is lost and in Me you must believe.
I'll forgive your sin's and from them set you free.

Whispers of Jesus I've heard them for a long, long time.
Some of his whispers, He has given me to put into rhyme.
I love to hear His voice speak, so soft and low.
In His likeness, I want my life always to show.

He whispers sweet words, in the stillness of the night.
I try to put them on paper, before the dawn's early light.
Sometimes the dawn of a new day comes into view,
Before the words He is whispering are completely through.

At times Jesus whispers His words into my ears,
Although I may have heard them before through the years.
Yet each time He whispers, it gives me great peace.
My faith in Him is sure to increase.

He whispers words of comfort, into my hungry soul.
His words of grace, love and mercy never grow old.
I could never put into words what His voice really means to me.
Soon He will whisper, "Come Home," then His face I'll see.

Thoughts Of Jesus And His Love

At the stars in the heavens tonight I have gazed,
My mind goes back to my childhood days.
God's great love to me He did show,
In His likeness I want always to grow.

Oh, how I love Him. He is my dearest friend,
I can always on Him truly depend.
He has forgiven me where I have failed,
Because to the cross His hand's were nailed.

He paid for my sin's with His precious blood;
Those terrible scars, I have never understood.
Yet God, the Father, gave Jesus His Son,
For us a home in heaven when this race is run.

As I sit here tonight with my mind upon Him,
Life is fast slipping by, the stars are growing dim.
Things of this world won't matter any more.
He is waiting for me on that heavenly shore.

There He will take me by he hand,
Saying, "Welcome home, my child, to God's fair land."
To those loved ones I leave here behind:
Don't weep for me, just bear me in mind.

3

Does your life measure up to God's command?
If He should call where do you stand?
Fall on your knees, before it's too late.
Ask God's forgiveness, your sins He will take.

There is always room at the foot of the cross.
God wants you to be saved, not forever lost.
There is no happier life you will find,
Oh, what peace and joy for your soul and mind.

 ## Prayers After Midnight

It's after midnight, two-thirty in the morning.
A closer walk with You, Jesus, I have a yearning.
I have been spending sometime in Your word,
Asking once again my prayers to be heard.

I love to talk to You, Jesus, in the quietness of the night.
I can feel Your presence, Your arms holding me tight.
I know you love me and will answer my prayers,
Regardless, day or night, anytime of the hour.

I gave You my children, when they were very small.
I know that You hear them, whenever they call.
I know someday you will take them to Heaven,
Because their hearts to You they have given.

As a young mother with children small,
Along came heartaches, I didn't heed God's call.
Although He has forgiven and brought me a long way
I shall always thank Him. I, too, had a debt to pay.

If I had listened more closely to His call,
I'm sure my life would have been worth more to all.
But my life is passing, growing closer to the end;
Jesus, take care of my family and in Heaven we will spend.

I feel I have failed them, while small, as well as grown.
I ask Your forgiveness, they have children of their own.
You see, I can't go back, not even for a day.
I still remember things I failed to do and say.

I thank You, God, for my children you have given.
Their health and happiness, please bring them to Heaven,
When our life down here shall come to an end,
With Jesus, family and loved ones eternity we will spend.

Jesus Save Our Families

Jesus, there are heartaches in our families' homes,
Some not living for You, in sin they roam.
My heart aches for each of them tonight.
Please, help them live for You, and do what's right.

You promised in Your word, You would save each one,
If I would live for You until my work here is done.
I have given each child and grandchild to You.
I know You will save each soul, too.

I will give You thanks for their souls tonight,
Knowing in my heart You will hold each one tight.
I will be there with You, in Heaven some day,
When You bring them home, forever to stay.

You have been telling me to put my house in order,
You are coming for me, try to work a little harder.
Do away with earthly things down here,
Get ready to leave family and friends, you love so dear.

Jesus, I'm going home to Heaven with You to live,
All of my heartaches to You I must give,
Will You take each one and answer prayer,
As I leave each one in Your loving care?

Walking With You Lord

By Velma Price Brookshire

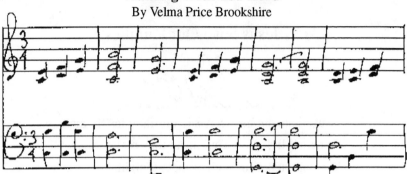

1. Walking with You, Lord, walking with You. In early
2. You helping me, Lord, watch all I do. Help me to

1. morning, and through the dew. Throughout the day hours,
2. walk, Lord, only with You. You holding my hand,

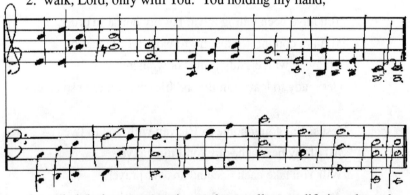

1. and nighttime, too, not just a short walk, - my lifetime through.
2. my friend so true, walking with You, Lord, walking with You.

Walking With You Lord (Continued)

3. You take my heartaches, carry them, too,

   The burdens grow lighter, as sun shines through.

   Your love seen by others, in all I do.

   Walking with You, Lord, walking with You.

4. We've walked over mountains, dark valleys gone through.

   There's no other friend in this world like You.

   You are my comfort, in times of sorrow,

   Walking with You, Lord, walking with You.

5. I know You love me, whatever I do.

   Wherever You lead me, I'll walk with You.

   Through heaven's gates, Lord, I want to go through,

   Walking with You, Lord, walking with You.

Jesus, Make Me More Like You

Dear Jesus, I am only a small piece of clay,
Mold me and make me, in Your own way.
Help me to always do and say the things that are right.
May the glow of Jesus shine through me bright.

I love you Jesus, Saviour and Lord.
Help me always to live with others, in one accord,
Never to say or do things that cause harm,
Only showing the love of Jesus so warm.

Telling them Jesus died to save them from sin,
Just open their heart's door and ask Him in.
He will forgive you, make your life clean.
You must put your faith in Jesus, in your heart believe.

You will find peace and contentment for a broken heart,
Even if it's been shattered and torn all apart.
There is nothing in this world my Savior cannot do,
Just believe in Him, He leaves it all up to you.

Jesus, is always just a prayer away,
Morning, noon or night, He will hear what you say.
While on my knees, in secret I steal away:
I know He will answer, when I humble pray.

He takes away the cares and woes of this life,
There are so many heartaches and troubles nigh.
God gave us His word, from His Holy Book.
To hide them in my heart, as on its pages I look.

Jesus, let me see Your face, where the blood ran down
From under the thorns, which was Your crown.
The scars in Your hands, once again let me see,
Reminding me how much You suffered to set me free.

Dear Jesus, draw me closer from day to day.
Don't let me forget the price You paid.
Helping me to live for You the rest of my life,
No matter how rough the road or dark the night.

Only the life I live for Jesus will last,
When my time here on earth has come to pass.
I pray You will take me to Heaven then,
To be with You dear Jesus, family, loved ones and friends.

Dreams Or Visions

I remember as a child being very sick in bed,
My mother, putting cold, wet cloths on my head.
As she sat by my bed that cold winter night,
Praying to Jesus I would be all right.

As I drifted into a restless sleep,
I saw a beautiful mansion on a hill so steep.
There were pretty flowers blooming everywhere,
So I started climbing the hill, trying to get near.

After I had gotten close, where I could see,
There was a fence around, tall as a tree.
With only one gate, to enter therein,
All of a sudden, I felt so alone then.

No one there to open the gate for me,
I thought, if only I could get inside, so I could see.
There on my hands and knees, I tried to crawl
Through under the fence, which looked so tall.

While on my hands and knees, trying to get through,
I cried out, "Please help, somebody! What must I do?"
When a still small voice spoke sweetly to me,
"Come unto me, I am the one who holds the key."

When I woke, the fever was gone,
My heart was broken, Mother still sat there alone.
Realizing then, it was Jesus, reminding me of my sin,
I must come through Jesus, if I wanted to get in.

At a young age, I opened my heart's door,
Asking Jesus' forgiveness, while kneeling on the floor.
In the little country church, where memories remain,
Jesus saved my soul, praise His Holy name.

Now I know there is a mansion waiting for me,
It wasn't a dream, it is real, you see.
For Jesus paid the price on Mount Calvary;
He built that mansion, it is all debt free.

Jesus Can Be Seen In A baby's Smile

Father, we give thanks for our children today,
The joy that fills our hearts, while watching them play.
Their smiling little faces are all aglow,
With the love of Jesus, to us they show.

Sometimes you can erase the outward expression.
By letting them see your very presence.
A baby is so innocent, beautiful, without and within,
As a baby born here on Earth, Jesus you began.

Jesus, You were living in Heaven long ago,
Then You came to Earth, Your love to show.
We must come to You, with childlike faith;
Then all of our sins and heartaches, You will take.

Please help us to remember, when we see a baby's smile,
We will know it's the love of Jesus in the child.
We know You can use children in every way,
To help us grow in love and not to stray.

Once again when we see our children smile,
May we see Your face, too, all the while.
They are little and throughout the years,
From baby to adults, for we love them so dear.

Help us to be the Mom and Dad, You would have us to be,
By telling them about Jesus, who died to set them free.
We need Your help, too, dear Jesus all the time,
That the love of Jesus on our faces will always shine.

God's Unseen Hands

Have you felt the touch of God's unseen hands?
When things go wrong, you don't understand,
You cannot see Him, but you know He is near,
Saying, "Place your hands in mine and have no fear."

Then all of a sudden, peace fills your heart,
The burden is lifted, you make a new start.
That's God's love and His unseen hands,
He reaches out to us, in this weary land.

The peace and joy, when His hands you can't see,
Yet the hands of God are as real as can be.
We cry out to Him, at day or in the night;
His hands of assurance hold us tight.

God has healing, in His tender hands,
He has love for all throughout the land.
There is saving power, for all of us,
Believing Jesus died and in Him we must trust.

We must be sorry for all of our sins,
Asking Jesus' forgiveness and live for Him then,
Yielding Him our hearts, body and soul,
Striving to win others, whether young or old.

While in His still, small voice to us He speaks,
I will be your strength when you are weak.
My unseen hands are always there,
Leading you home to Heaven so fair.

As an earthly father takes his child by the hand,
Saying, "Hold tight my child," in tender command.
Our heavenly Father does for us even more,
He walks the dark valleys and along the shores.

Those nail-scarred hands, in my mind can see,
Those scars are there because of you and me.
How could He have loved us so very much?
Oh, those Hands of God have such gentle a touch.

So when things go wrong and seem useless, too,
He reaches out those unseen hands to you,
Take hold once again and hold on tight,
He will open Heaven's doors and pour out new light.

Showing you things you've never seen,
When totally on Him you have leaned.
Just stay close to Him and in His word,
Souls will be saved, who have never heard.

Those unseen hands, are oh, so precious to me,
They saved me from sin and set me free.
Yet things still happen I don't understand,
He still reaches down and takes me in His unseen hand.

Little Prayers

Another night of restlessness, with my mind upon Thee,
I am so thankful to God for setting me free.
Some of my loved ones aren't living for Him, I am told,
Oh, how I long to see them safe in God's fold.

The nights are so long, but Jesus is near,
I can always feel His presence here.
As I lift my hands to give Him praise,
Through tear-dimmed eyes, I sometimes gaze.

I love Him and thank Him for what He has done
For me, my family and my loved ones.
Not one lost soul, I pray there will be,
But all will be in Heaven, with Jesus and me.

Jesus died for all, shed His precious blood, you see,
When He hung upon the cross on Mount Calvary.
My prayers are to be like Him each day that I live,
May others see Jesus in me and their hearts to Him give.

I know I have failed Him by things done and said,
Also, not going and doing things where He has led.
I pray, God forgive me, I have grieved His heart so,
Help me to live a life your love to others show.

If I could go back to a little girl at the age of nine,
There I met Jesus not a doubt in my mind.
He forgave me of my sins I felt were many,
There He came into my heart, not remembering any.

Oh, what a Savior, God's precious son,
Why can't you see just what He has done?
His blood He shed on Mount Calvary,
Paying the price just for you and me.

Jesus My Master

Master, am I more like You today than yesterday?
Help me in this life, to watch what I say.
Make me more like You, I beg You please,
A blessing to You and others, I want to be.

More like You, Master, I long to be,
Walking hand-in-hand, that others might see
A likeness of You, in my life and face,
That they might know Your amazing grace.

Master, teach me to lift up Your name each day,
Watching careful, things I do along the way.
My life is an open book, before the world,
Weary darts of Satan, sometimes at me are hurled.

As the disciples ask, "Master, teach us to pray,"
Fill me with Your Holy Spirit and love each day.
May we walk together, You be my friend,
Whom have known each other since my life began.

There is nothing more sweeter than my Master's voice,
As He speaks to me, He gives me a choice.
To listen, to pray, to heed and obey,
Or turn my back and go my own way.

There will be a day of regret, if I don't heed,
There will be trials and troubles, and Him I will need.
So I will cling ever closer, to my Master's hand,
As He leads me daily through this weary land.

My Master grows sweeter as the days go by,
He lives in my heart, forever to abide.
He listens when I am down, sad or blue,
He will walk with me through dark valleys, too.

Master, You love me so much, You gave Your life,
You have been my help, through troubles and strife.
Master, I would be willing, for others to die,
If You needed me, and never asking why.

Is Jesus your Master, Savior, Friend?
If you searched the world over, to its very end?
Could you find any other, which to compare?
He gave His life on Calvary, because He cared.

His grace, salvation, love, peace and joy,
He gave freely to all, you can't buy, steal or borrow.
My heart's desire each day and hour,
Make me more like You, Master, is my prayer.

Sweet Voice Of Jesus

The sweet voice of Jesus spoke to me one day,
Saying, "Come unto me, I'll take your sins away."
I fell on my knees, He heard my prayer,
Forgiving and saving my soul that very hour.

Have you heard Jesus' sweet voice today,
Did you read His Word, did you pray,
Did you shut the world out of your mind?
Tell Jesus you love Him, then listen sometime.

His voice is a soft whisper, sweet and clear,
But you must listen with your heart's ears.
With your thoughts upon Him and His word,
Prayerful, in the stillness His voice can be heard.

No other voice speaks so tender and so soft,
It will cause you to think back to the old rugged cross.
Jesus said, "Father, forgive them, they know not what they do."
There Jesus gave GOD back His spirit, for me and you.

I love to hear his sweet voice whisper, so soft and low,
While walking by His side, and in His shadow,
Him holding my hand tight, as He talks with me,
Strolling the streets of glory, we soon shall be.

Talking To Jesus

While waiting for the breaking of a new dawn,
I've been talking to Jesus, wondering how long
Before friends and family will join God's fold?
I have trusted them all to Jesus, in His arms to hold.

I give you thanks, dear Jesus, for I do believe
Your word is true; You have proved it to be.
Although Satan has often tried to deceive,
Jesus will always be Jesus, can't you see?

We must live for Him and read His word,
There might be some who have never heard.
Asking Jesus to forgive them and never doubt,
Those living in sin, Jesus will bring them out.

Someday, taking us all to Heaven to live with Him,
We will sing a new song, a brand-new hymn.
God's glory forever will shine so bright,
Jesus is the light, there will be no night.

Our lives here on Earth are an open book.
Each day we live, God always looks:
Has the blood of Jesus, covered your life's page?
Or is there still sin from beginning of age?

God knows all the heartaches, and shares a part.
He is the only one, who understands a broken heart,
Which has been tattered and torn from life's past.
Yes, His love covers all, and forever will last.

God gave Heaven's best, His only Son,
To this cruel sinful world, Jesus did come.
He bled and died, upon the rugged cross,
To set us free from sin, there He paid the cost.

Oh, how I love Him, He is my Saviour so true.
To Heaven someday He will take me. What about you?
Have you asked His forgiveness for your sins?
Why not open your heart's door and ask Him in?

Time is slipping by so very fast.
Jesus will forgive you of all your past,
The present, the future, please make haste.
Ask Jesus into your heart today, why do you wait?

The love of Jesus can change your heart,
Give Him your life and make a new start.
Until you trust Him, you will never know,
God's love to others through you will show.

Dear Jesus, my loved ones and friends are in your care,
Will you love them for me, and their burden's bear?
Saving their souls, and to Heaven bring,
For eternity we will praise You, our Saviour, Lord and King.

In Need Of Someone To Pray

Lonely and sad came a voice over the phone,
What's wrong in your life, are you lonesome for home?
Do you need a friend or loved one to pray?
I just wanted to hear your voice, I heard them say.

Has Jesus laid a lost soul upon your mind?
They could have been a friend or child of yours or mine.
May we always be prayerful and listen with the heart,
Before we ever speak or dare to start.

Let us be sure we have God's Holy Spirit to teach
Us to listen, to read His word and others may we reach.
Jesus, who died for me, died for others, too,
If it means I must pray for them the whole night through.

Lord, lay some soul upon my heart today,
For you to save their souls before it's too late.
Lord keep me, filling me with your love and power,
That I might reach others for you any time day, night or hour.

Pray For Our Teens

There is a sadness in my heart tonight,
For our lost teens to find Jesus as their light.
Darkness holds nothing good for our teens of this word,
Satan is stealing the souls of our boys and girls.

Please! You who know Jesus will you really pray,
That from sin they will turn their lives away?
Crying out to Jesus their sins to forgive,
Asking Him into their hearts and for Him live.

If they only knew the peace and contentment they will find,
For their lives, bodies, souls and minds.
Drugs and drinking can never do the part,
What God can do for a broken and tattered heart.

He can save your soul wash your heart pure and clean.
Believe in Him, trusting Him and totally on Him lean.
Jesus can set you free from any kind of sin and lust,
You must put your life in His hands, with full trust.

Little Birds

Have you ever watched the little birds fly through the air?
The red bird pick seed from the garden sunflower?
Have you wondered by whom they are cared?
Feeding on seed, bugs, worms and all are shared.

Our Heavenly Father, watches over all of them,
Total trust is put in Him.
They have knowledge of where to look for food,
Where to take shelter, when weather isn't good.

Have you seen the little robin, with a broken wing?
Hopping on the ground, she doesn't even sing.
Trying to find food, just to stay alive,
Waiting for her wing to heal, so she can fly.

Our heavenly Father watches over all of them,
While the sun is shining or the stars are growing dim.
He shelters the little ones from all harm,
As He spreads out His protecting arms.

Our heavenly Father will do the same for us,
When we in Him have put our trust.
The lilies of the valley grow at His command,
He too will hold you in His loving hands.

God's Hand Painted Leaves

Fall is a beautiful time of the year,
God's art and hand paintings everywhere.
Who but God could paint so beautiful a world?
He colors the leaves, even makes the wind whirl.

People have tried to paint God's world of art,
No one can compare, not just a small part.
God's art was the first from beginning of time,
He spoke it all into place, with His word and rhyme.

He gave the leaves their bright colors back then
He has known when to turn their colors since time began.
Mixing them all together, red, yellow, pink, tan and rust,
As the cool breeze blows, from dawn until dusk.

The beautiful leaves will soon fall to the ground,
Some will be raked, some are left lying all around.
As they decay, going back to mother earth,
When spring comes again, God will give new birth.

The sap will rise, new growth will appear,
When they begin to bud, you know spring is near.
This is God's hand painting of life year-by-year,
Listen! the singing of the birds, you can hear.

Leaves will turn green, swaying in the summer breeze,
As summer passes, keep our eyes upon the leaves.
They are waiting for the World's Greatest Artist, so dear,
As the leaves start changing you will know He has appeared.

The Beauty In The Clover Blossom

Let me see the beauty in the clover blossom that my
    grandchildren see,
As they gather them in their little hands, giving them to me,
Saying, "I have pretty flowers for you Grandma B."
With happy smiles on their faces, as they show their love for me.

Taking the small blossoms, I put them into a vase.
As I add water, I study each little face.
Thinking to myself, to a child these are as pretty as a rose,
How happy they have made me, you will never know.

Let us not forget to tell the children thank you and I love you,
For they need to be loved, and you will hear them say "I love
    you, too."
The pale-colored blossoms on tiny green stems –
Jesus, let me see the beauty my grandchildren see in them.

Children see the small things God has made so beautiful.
Their faces all aglow and hearts with love so full,
As I look at the tiny clover blossoms, some still in my hand,
Thanking God for the beauty He gives throughout the land.

There were lots of clover blossoms picked by their little hands,
Given to Grandpa B. and I, with love which God understands.
Our grandchildren are truly a blessing to each of us,
I pray their little hearts will someday in Jesus trust.

The children have gone home now, I'm still amazed,
I picked more clover blossoms and under a magnifying glass I
    gazed.
Each little tiny part reminds me of a lily in bloom,
Heads looking upward, colors blending of white, pink, purple
    and maroon.

All bonded together to form a beautiful blossom,
What I have learned from the clover bloom will never be
    forgotten,
I want to say thank you, Jesus, and children, for letting me see
The beauty in the clover blossoms they have given to me.

For my grandchildren Robby, Danny and Joey Quillen

Written August, 1994

31

Birthdays

Birthdays are stepping stones to Heaven,
I thank God for each one He has given.
Do you realize, if there were no stepping stones,
Our life would be over, we would be home.

God gives some people lots of birthdays,
Others aren't so lucky, they have shorter days.
Jesus needed some people to join Him up there,
In beautiful Heaven, so wondrously fair.

As you celebrate your special day,
Stop and give Jesus thanks, along the way.
May He give you grace for many more,
Walking beside you, until you reach Heaven's shore.

Someday we will step on the last stepping stone,
But as we walk, we are not alone.
Our Jesus walks with us, day and night,
He is the way the truth and light.

Who Are We To Judge

Are you sure you are saved? In your life it doesn't show.
Did you give your heart to Jesus? Your life hasn't grown.
Let us not ask so many questions and only pray,
That God will keep them and not let them stray.

Let us hold other Christians, especially those who are new,
Up before God in prayers the whole day through.
It's hard to grow in Jesus, when no one prays for you,
Satan finds so many faults in everything we do.

So let us not judge others but look at the life we live.
Does it reflect the life of Jesus, did our all to Him give?
For someday as we stand before God's judgement throne,
He will judge our life by His very own.

Worry

My dear sisters and brothers in Jesus,
Let's not let things any longer hinder us.
So set your minds at ease, don't worry another day,
Who knows? God may have planned things this way.

Maybe someone will ask Jesus into their heart,
While reading the poem and make a new start.
I know God will work it all out somehow,
Let us concentrate on Him, forgetting problems for now.

May God give many souls for your labor,
We have so many lost families, friends and neighbors.
I pray God will bring us closer to Him each day,
And may others see Jesus in us each step of life's way.

Not one soul crossed our path that we haven't asked,
Do you know Jesus? It's not an easy task.
Our days are going by fast, souls are slipping away,
I want to hear Jesus say, "Well done" someday.

So, dear sisters and brothers, I'm praying for you,
Many souls to be saved before life here is through.
Now let us take hold of His hand and hold on tight,
Then we won't have to worry anymore, right!

Wrong Decisions

I know my life has been a failure,
Where the things of God are concerned.
God showed me a special person,
When I was very young.

I was saved at he age of nine,
Walked closely to Jesus all the time.
He was my special friend and playmate,
At my make-believe table, He always dined.

I have often wondered, does God really
Take our failures and turn them into good?
What would my life truly have been like,
If I had listened and obeyed Him like I should?

Time has come and gone by now,
My hair has turned to gray.
Dear Jesus, I am so sorry,
What else now can I say?

We should always be on our guard,
Because Satan is sure to trick us.
If we don't stay on our knees and in God's word,
Our life on this Earth will sure be a mix-up.

I'm Just What God Made Me

Each tiny baby born into this world
Is a gift from heaven, whether boy or girl.
They are given to us from God above
To teach and train each day with love.

God gives each child its very own features;
He is the Master of all creation and teacher.
He knows what each one need and feel inside;
In our hearts He wants to always abide.

Little girls are special, in God's eyes.
When we look into the mirror we must realize
I'm what God made me, I'm beautiful as can be.
I'm different from all others like God made me.

I may have some resemblance of Daddy and Mother
Of my sister and relatives or others.
If God made everyone to look the same,
How would we tell them apart, regardless their names?

My actions and ways might differ from others
Yet, I'm made in God's image, not any other.
People only see what I see, when I look into the mirror –
A face, eyes, nose, mouth, head with hair and two ears.

God sees my heart and hears my every cry,
Doesn't matter how I look or the color of my eyes.
Little girls are beautiful, yet different as can be,
I look different from all others, just like God made me.

I have a sister a little older than me,
We don't look much alike, it's easy to see.
I love her she is different and special, too;
God made her different just like me and you.

Mother and Daddy love us both the same,
Doesn't matter the age, looks or the name.
Each person I see has a different expression,
Some smile or frown and from others, laughs are expected.

I practice my music, giggle and laugh, tease and clown around,
Do my chores, swim, climb, my feet hardly stay on the ground,
I'm happy-go-lucky, in Jesus I've been set free,
I'm beautiful. I'm just what God made me.

For a Special Little Girl Teresa Jansen
Written June 5, 1994

Mama, Tell Me About Jesus

A little boy climbed upon his Mama's knees,
Saying, "Mama, Mama please tell me.
Does Jesus live within your hearts?
Is He there to stay, never to part?

"Please tell me about Jesus," I heard him say.
"Do you really know Him, will you teach me to pray?"
"Some other time, my son, we will have a long talk,
Right now, it's time for me to take my walk."

His little face became sad, with tears in his eyes,
Walking slowly outside, he began to cry.
Asking, "Jesus, where are you? I really want to know.
Please, someone, the way to Jesus to me show."

"My Mama doesn't know Him or won't take the time,
To read the Bible to me, not even a nursery rhyme.
She says she has too much work to do,
Dinner to cook and the dishes when through."

To himself thinking, I wonder if my little friend
Will take me to Sunday school this weekend?
Maybe there I will find the Jesus man.
Down to his friend's house away he ran.

At his friend's house the children were all at play,
His heart needed answers, so he didn't stay.
"I want to find Jesus, doesn't anyone care?
Just a Bible verse or two, with me share?

"I know, I'll go to Grandma's, I'm sure she knows
The way to find Jesus, to me she will show."
On down the street again he ran, knocking on her door,
Sweet voice saying, "Come in, my child," like always before.

With a smile on his face, climbing upon Grandma's knees,
Saying, "Grandma, Grandma, please tell me,
Does Jesus live within your heart?"
Reaching for her worn and tattered Bible, her hand did start.

Opening God's word to Matthew 1:16, with pride –
*Joseph the husband of Mary, of whom was born Jesus, who is
        called Christ.*
She also read John 3:16 with love in her voice,
Saying, "My child, God gives to us a choice."

John 3:16, *For God so loved the world, that he gave his only
begotten Son, that whosoever believeth in him should not perish,
but have everlasting life.*

Revelations 3:20, *Behold I stand at the door and knock,*
Sitting there in her old rocking chair, she begins to rock.
*If any man hear my voice and open the door,
I will come in to him.* Yes, my child, He will live forever more.

And will sup with him, and he with me.
Do you understand what I have read, now do you see?
The way to find Jesus in right here in His word,
With faith believing in Jesus, now you have heard.

Open your heart's door, in faith ask Jesus in.
He will come in and save you from your sins,
Filling your heart with His spirit and His love,
Giving you a home in Beautiful Heaven above.

Putting his arms around Grandma's neck, giving her a kiss,
Saying, "I love you, Grandma, now Heaven I won't miss.
I must go tell Mama and Daddy, I found Jesus today,
He lives in my heart now, forever to stay."

Rushing out the door, running up the street
In front of his house I heard a loud screech.
While he was crossing the street, a car came hurrying by,
Not seeing him in time, I then heard him cry.

It was too late now, Mama came running out to see.
The little boy lay quiet there in the street,
As his Mama knelt down, she heard him faintly say,
"Don't worry Mama. Tell Daddy I found Jesus today."

Memories

On August the twenty-fifth, nineteen hundred ninety-one,
I relived a lifetime before the setting of the sun.
I went back once more to the old home place,
Happy memories in my mind I began to retrace.

The old log house burned down several years ago;
Another one stands in it's place for show.
The inside isn't finished, it's only a shell;
It may never be finished, is what the neighbors tell.

As I look about, things aren't the same today.
No one lives there, no children to run and play.
Cattle roam the hillsides, and daily feed
On the tall green grass and all the weeds.

I can remember sitting on my mother's knees,
When just a small child of two or three,
Her telling me about Jesus and His love,
His coming down from Heaven up above.

Born in a manger, His bed was of hay;
God sent Him to Earth, our debt to pay.
He gave up His life, for you and for me,
While dying upon a cross to set us free.

At the old family alter before going to bed,
Daddy would take the Bible and the word was read.
Then kneeling there before the open fire,
They poured out their hearts to Jesus there.

Many times as a child, while I was outside at play,
I could hear my mother's voice as she would pray.
She prayed for her family, also others;
She prayed for her sister and two brothers.

Always, while the chores were being done,
Songs about Jesus were daily sung.
Once again, she would steal away some place in prayer,
Telling Jesus her troubles and heartaches there.

Jesus, take care of my children, please save their souls,
Save them while young, don't wait until they are old.
It might be too late then, I would hear her say,
This was her prayer, from morning until end of day.

I can remember walking to Sunday school,
We would go every Sunday, that was the rule,
Unless we were sick, or the weather was too bad;
If I had to miss, it made my heart sad.

Revival meetings were held in the spring and in the fall,
Those times were very special to us all.
People would come from everywhere
To hear God's Word preached loud and clear.

We walked through the rain and through the snow,
At night Daddy carried a lantern, our way to show.
Sometimes he would carry me on his shoulders,
Until I could see to walk by myself and was older.

Then came a still, small voice speaking to me,
"Your soul is lost, I came to set you free."
At the little country church, I knelt in prayer,
Jesus forgave my sins while I was kneeling there.

I can still hear my dear mother shouting God's praise,
With the glory of Heaven shining on her face.
That night is still fresh in my mind yet today,
When at the age of nine, Jesus washed my sins away.

As time races through my mind again,
I've grown a little older, maybe ten.
A family moves away, new ones move in,
New babies are born, and I make new friends.

The Burketts, Hamblens, Manis's and Prices, too,
Jones, Davis, Cope, Carver's, Shanks and who?
Could you remember all, when so small?
Oh, yes, Rippetoe, Bookers, Paynes, Williams and Halls.

Elkins, Byrds, Brooks, Lawsons, Klepper and Frost.
Some have gone on before us, I pray not lost;
Harrells, McDonalds, Gladsons and Lees,
In Heaven someday, again I hope to see.

There were the Goforths, Heltons and Woods,
I sure can't remember now, like once I could:
Yes, the Bowlins, Jinks, Stipes, Jaynes, and Hardens,
Courtneys, Brewers, if I've forgotten anyone, I beg your pardon.

The old Choptack school house is torn away,
A cemetery now, our loved ones lay beneath the clay.
Part of my family have gone on before,
I'll meet them someday on that beautiful shore.

We drove then to Clouds Creek, just for a look,
Passing homes where friends once lived by God's book.
They would walk to revivals then, didn't matter how far,
In wagons or on horseback, if they didn't own a car.

Then on to Lakeview where another old schoolhouse sits,
With windows broken out, door wide open now is
Destruction to the old building by others befall;
Happy memories there, too, of friends I recall.

Christmas plays about Jesus, they stay in my mind,
Many friends there, too, I had to leave behind.
I often wonder, Where have they all gone?
Then I ask "Jesus, Are they in Heaven, our home?

There was another little schoolhouse, named Marble Hall,
We walked there sometimes to play baseball.
The place now where it once stood,
Is all grown over with grass, weeds and woods.

We drove up U.S. 11, where I had walked lots of times,
Spending time with aunts, uncles and cousins of mine.
We then stopped to visit another cousin, you see,
I had stopped before, but gone he would be.

This day was a special day in my life:
He told me about Jesus Saving him one night.
I was a night of revival at Choptack again,
Where we were forgiven of all our sins.

Danney Bentley, and G.D. Barrette preached God's word,
About the blood of Jesus as it was never heard,
How Jesus bled and died for you and for me,
We can be born again from sin set free.

My cousin Mack said, "I can still see your face aglow.
Oh, how the love of Jesus on it did show,
You came to me, your hand on my head did lay,
The power from Heaven fell, filling my heart to stay."

Shouting and praises to God did ring out,
As the answers to prayers of God's people came about.
What happy and joyous times; in those days,
Christians were not ashamed to give God praise.

Today in our churches if someone says amen,
Some will look at you as if you had sinned.
Churches are just buildings, although some stand tall;
God has withdrawn His spirit, they are beginning to fall.

The trip for the day ended back at Thelma's.
She, Eva and I the whole day did ramble,
From Kingsport, Choptack, Clouds Creek and to
Lakeview, Rogersville and home. Gee! I'm tired, aren't you?

Dear Jesus, please make me more like You,
That You in my life others could see, too.
We are here in this world just a short stay,
To always love others and for them to pray.

I have wondered from time to time, since that day,
Was there someone I failed to help find their way?
The past had gone now; it's too late, I can't go back;
I want to always tell others about Jesus, who crosses my path.

Written Friday, August 30th, 1991
By Velma Price Brookshire

Friends, Eva Allen
Thelma Richardson

Memories Of Daddy

Thinking back to my childhood days,
Remembering Daddy and his happy face,
I first recall I was only two or three
At the old family altar, there on his knees.

Daddy would read the Bible to us at night,
As we sat by the open fire and the oil lamp light.
Then on their knees, Daddy and Mama knelt,
As they prayed for their family, love was felt.

I can remember sitting on Daddy's knee,
Him telling how much Jesus loves me.
Sister, brother, Daddy and Mama so dear,
Oh, how I have missed them through the years.

I had one sister and two brothers,
I am the youngest of the others.
Daddy loved us all, each one the same,
There wasn't any difference, regardless the name.

There was one Christmas, special to me,
With a little story book, under the tree.
It told about Jesus, born long ago,
In a manger in Bethlehem, for God loves us so.

I still have the little story book,
On it worn and tattered pages I've often looked.
I thank God for a Daddy who really cared,
And for the love of Jesus, with me shared.

We would go to Church and Sunday school,
Every Sunday morning, was always the rule.
Bible stories about Jesus to us were told,
I've never forgotten, they have never grown old.

Those happy days, when revival meetings were held,
God's word was preached and His power felt.
Young and old came and were gloriously saved.
Hands lifted toward Heaven, giving God Praise.

I gave my heart to Jesus at the age of nine,
My life has never been the same since that night.
The little country church in Choptack Tennessee,
Holds happy memories there, where Jesus found me.

Daddy worked very hard on the farm,
Also teaching us children, right from wrong.
He did all the work, with horses and by hand,
Never owned a tractor to till the land.

Seeing Daddy's hands in the fall of the year,
Cracked and sore from gathering corn by the ear.
No machinery to do all the hard part,
Working from dawn until dusk, never losing heart.

He gathered the corn and the wheat, put up the hay,
Times were really hard, you worked without much pay.
As I got older, I, too, worked in the field,
Step after step, following behind my Daddy's heels.

I am so thankful today, for the Christian home,
For the old log house, without a phone.
We carried the water from the spring or well,
Chopped the wood, neighbors came by to sit a spell.

Stories of hard times were really true back then,
We had no car, very little money to spend.
Yet Jesus lived deep inside of each heart,
When someone was sick, everyone took part.

The women cooked and brought in the food,
Men fed the cattle and chopped the wood.
Love of Jesus showed in their lives back then.
Will times ever be like that again?

Daddy's gone home now, to Heaven above.
With Jesus, Mama, Sister and Brother, we love.
Just one brother and I are left, you see,
Time is passing by fast, for him and for me.

For you who have daddies still living today,
Please take time, just once to say;
"Daddy I love you," before it's too late,
For God may call you or him at any date.

Be sure you both know Jesus, too,
He bled and died for each of you.
In faith believing, open your heart's door,
Ask Jesus in to live forever more.

Someday in Heaven, we all shall be,
Daddy, Mama, Sister, Brothers and me,
Never, no never, to be apart again,
Singing, *Glory hallelujah to Jesus, our Lord and King.*

In loving memory of my Daddy, Andrew G. Price

by Velma Price Brookshire
June 12, 1992

MEMORIES OF MY PRECIOUS MOTHER

The first memory I recall of being in this world,
I was a very small tow-headed little girl.
I wasn't very old, I'm sure not even three,
These are the memories of my precious Mother and me.

It was a beautiful summer sun-shiny day.
I suppose I was dirty, from being at play.
She had bathed me in the old wash tub,
She dried me so gently with every rub.

I recall sitting quietly, there on her knees,
Her telling me how much Jesus loves me.
Your body belongs to Jesus, you are His child,
He wants to live in your heart for a long while.

I can hear her sweet voice say,
As she prayed to Jesus day after day.
Please Jesus, save my family, they are yours, you see,
These are the memories of my precious mother and me.

I can recall her rocking me to sleep, in the old rocking chair,
As she sang songs of Jesus and stroked my hair.
A loving smile on her face, always would be,
These are the memories of my precious mother and me.

The Bible was read by Daddy each night,
As we sat by the open fire and the old lamp light.
There they knelt on their knees, to God in prayer,
Pouring out their burdens to Jesus there.

Mother made me pretty dresses, from the new feed sacks,
Mending other clothes with love, every stitch she tacked.
My stockings were always mended, for my little feet,
Besides the cooking and baking, we had plenty to eat.

I was always told with love her good advice,
While telling me things not to do, which wasn't nice.
I never heard a dirty word nor words of slang,
Ever uttered from her lips, she honored God's name.

As a child, I can remember my Mother praying,
All through the day, while I was outside playing.
She sang songs of Jesus, always happy as could be,
These are the memories of my precious mother and me.

To church each Sunday and to Sunday school,
She was a Godly mother, who lived by His rules,
Telling me always about Jesus and His love,
The mansion, He has for us in Heaven above.

Jesus found me and saved my soul, at the age of nine,
My life has never been the same since that night.
I can hear my mother, shouting God's praise,
She and others, with hands toward Heaven raised.

I still have the last dolly she gave me,
Early one morning, she put it under the Christmas tree.
It has blond hair, will open and close its eyes.
When you turn her on her face, she really cries.

Out of the old catalog, she ordered it from Sears,
I've loved it and kept it, all through these years.
What a happy and merry Christmas, back in Tennessee,
These are the memories of my precious mother and me.

Do you have memories of a Christian mother and dad?
So many don't have and it makes my heart sad.
Once again I say, "Thank You Dear Jesus,"
For memories of a precious mother who loved us.

Tonight Mother is with Jesus, giving Him praise,
I can still hear her praying for the children she raised.
Knowing someday in Heaven we all will be,
What happy memories of my precious mother and me.

Thanks once again, Jesus, for memories of my dear mother,
There will never, never be another,
Who could take her place or love me, you see?
These are the memories of my precious mother and me.

In Memory Of My Precious Mother
Cora Lee "Lawson" Price
April 20, 1993

What Is A Friend?

A friend is someone you meet along life's way,
Someone who cares if you have heartaches night or day.
They hold you close to God in their prayers,
Never forgetting the heavy burden's you bare.

They are always aware of your needs each day,
When heartaches come, they are there to stay,
They may have traveled the same road in the past,
Knowing only the love of Jesus, will truly last.

I met a young Christian eleven years ago,
A broken heart and loneliness in his face did show.
I was a stranger standing outside, looking in,
But I felt a tug at my heart, he needed a friend.

At Bethany Bible Church, he spoke of the potters wheel.
I knew in my heart, he wanted to do God's will,
Torn between a broken heart and the call of God in his life,
I prayed God's call would be the strongest amidst the strife.

Ever so often God brings someone to my mind,
I know I must pray, regardless the time.
There is a need somewhere, in their life to be met,
"Please, dear Jesus, others don't EVER let me forget."

In my heart some hold a special place.
Jesus, will you remember each face?
There is a friend who sticketh closer than a brother,
"That is Jesus," there will never be another.

A true friend is worth more than silver and gold,
A person with whom you can share the burdens of your soul,
Knowing, the only one you will ever tell,
Is Jesus, our savior, who knows us oh so well.

What Is A Prayer?

Do you suppose God ever wonders why we always ask,

Father, would you do this? Oh, please do that!

We, as people, like to be told by others we are loved,

Let's put self aside and love our Heavenly Father above.

Sharing Childhood Memories

The good times we shared about our childhood days,
No one could ever erase those memories away.
School days, play, work, church and revival times,
Are written deep inside of your soul and mine.

Yesterday, we relived only part of our young lives,
Because of our Christian parents who started the ties.
They taught us right from wrong and to always think of others,
Godly parents who loved us, our daddies and saintly mothers.

I've cherished my friends from childhood days,
Time has gone by now, my hair has turned gray.
I pray my life hasn't darkened not one path,
And because of my life God will hold back some of His wrath.

As we pray for those friends from our school days,
Who doesn't know Jesus nor walk in His way.
He will hear our prayers and save each soul,
Before their life ends, for we are growing old.

The Beauty Of The Dogwood Tree

Did you notice the beauty of God's handiwork this Spring?
Listen to the birds, how happily they sing.
Beauty of the flowers, the pink and white dogwood trees,
While looking at them, I thought how beautiful Heaven must be.

The grass and the trees are such a pretty shade of green,
God's handiwork, everywhere to be seen.
The clouds carry the rain to give them drinks,
The sunshine gives them growth and gives them strength.

Today, I gathered a bouquet of lilac and white dogwood,
The fragrance of the lilac smelled so sweet and good.
After a while, the dogwood blossoms bowed their heads,
I thought of Jesus hanging on the cross in my stead.

Have you noticed how a beautiful flower will wilt and die?
They bow their heads, as if to cry.
Yet, God made all things, some will live again.
Lifting up their heads, they will live again come Spring.

Jesus walked the rough road up Calvary Hill,
Knowing when He reached the top, scripture would be fulfilled.
There once again He asked God the Father to forgive,
Their sins, yours and mine, and in Heaven with Him live.

Again I was reminded that Jesus still lives,
So will the dogwood tree, new life Jesus will give.
As you look at the peddles of the pretty white blooms,
The red spots remind me of His death and the tomb.

Some people say, it was from the dogwood His cross was made,
After the cross, in a lonely tomb He was laid.
After three days, the grave could no longer keep Him there,
He is alive in Heaven, interceding for us, because He cares.

At the right of the Father, our Savior now sits,
Praying the road to Heaven, we won't miss.
It is straight and narrow, but Jesus will walk with us,
Believing He died, rose again, in Him we must trust.

Each time you see the flowers of a dogwood in bloom,
Just think if it wasn't for Jesus, our soul would be doomed.
God gave His only Son, that we might be free,
He died on the cross, which could have been The Dogwood Tree.

The Early Morning

It was early morning on that wonderful day,
When the angels came and rolled the stone away,
They have taken my Lord away, Mary cried,
As she wiped the tears from her eyes.

Jesus said, "Weep no more I'm here alive.
And will soon ascend unto my Father in the sky."
Yes, Jesus had risen from the grave,
Saying to his friends, "Fear not, be brave."

Today, I give my heavenly Father glory and praise,
For Jesus, from the grave He did raise.
He sits by the side of our Father there,
In Heaven, so beautiful and wondrously fair.

He Would Rise

It was for our sins our Savior did die,
He gave His life back to God, yes, for you and I.
They carried Him away after taking Him from the cross,
Put Him into a lowly grave which was for naught.

He told Mary and the disciples he would rise again,
But as the stone closed the grave, their faith seemed in vain.
On the third day Mary and Martha came at early dawn,
Seeing the stone rolled away and their Savior was gone.

Wondering where could he be, Mary heard someone speak,
It was Jesus speaking, they no longer had for him to seek.
The same sweet voice whispered, she soon recognized,
Just like He had promised her, from the grave He would rise.

Jesus' Garment Hem

As you travel life's road from dawn until end of day,
Did you tell someone about Jesus along the way?
Was there a word of love and cheer spoken to them?
Have you yourself, touched Jesus's garment hem?

Touching the hem of Jesus' garment can make a great change
In your life and mine, if we ask in His name.
He knows and cares, when we strive to touch His garment hem
And through faith believing we can touch Him.

Each day goes by we are closer to that wonderful day
When He will call our souls away.
Are you ready to meet Jesus face-to-face?
Have you touched His garment, do you know His saving grace?

You will know if you have touched Him,
Although at times your faith my grow dim,
Always keep reaching out to Him,
He will wrap you in His love and His garment hem.

Let Us Give Thanks

It will soon be Christmas, we will celebrate Jesus' birth.
We must sing praises to Jesus, throughout all the Earth.
Praising Him for His birth and the cross,
For without His birth and the cross we would be lost.

Not forgetting the tomb and His resurrection.
Praise God for our risen Lord.

Beauty

Beauty is within the depth of one's soul.
It can be possessed by both young and old,
Not the outward beauty of body and face,
It is Jesus living in the heart of every race.

He Gave His Life

While hanging upon the cross the heavens did know
Jesus was dying for the world's lost souls.
He paid the cost by giving up His life,
The soldiers didn't kill Him, although they tried.

THANKSGIVING

T-----Is for a time for giving Thanks.

H-----Is for the Happiness it brings.

A-----Is for the Answered prayers.

N-----Is for our Nice friends and Neighbors.

K-----Is for the Kindness they have shown.

S-----Is for our Blessed Savior.

G-----Is for His life He gave.

I-----Is for Into my heart He came.

V-----Is for Victory over the grave.

I-----Is for Impossible to please God, without faith.

N-----Is Never forgetting others.

G-----Is for Giving thanks in all things.

Each day we live should be a day of Thanksgiving

Christmas Is Coming

It's two-thirty in the morning,
The stars are shining bright.
As I think of Christmas coming,
All the pretty decorations and colored lights.

Then I pause, wondering what do people worship?
It's only a time for gifts and pleasure.
They never give Jesus any thought,
For it's Heaven that holds all the treasures.

Jesus, you were born a tiny baby,
From Heaven's glory You were sent.
God the Father loves us so,
Your death on the cross for us was spent.

You were always about Your Father's business,
As a little boy just twelve years of age.
You were so wise and eager to listen,
From the prophets of old, the laws of every page.

Although Mary and Joseph missed you,
Looking for You throughout the crowd.
Could they have really known the future,
The problems from the people You would have?

I have often wondered what You did,
The years untold of Your young life.
Where were You? Alone with God someplace,
Preparing for all of Your trouble and strife?

It's so lonely without You, Jesus,
Oh, the love and peace You can give.
Your protecting eye's always upon us,
Guiding us on our way to Heaven.

Again, as I think of Christmas,
As a little girl I will always remember.
There might have been one tiny toy,
Under the tree on Christmas morn.

Oh, the love of a Christian mom and dad,
Who told me what Christmas really meant.
They showed me love and were never sad,
That Jesus from Heaven, God did send.

Oh, yes I had two brothers and one sister, too.
They were all older, but they all knew,
Christmas was Jesus' time of year
To thank God for Jesus and blessings, never few.

God has blessed us with health and food,
A roof over our heads throughout the year.
What else could we have asked for so good?
Than the love of God and answered prayer.

I still have my little story book,
My daddy gave me one Christmas morn.
It tells me about Jesus, as on its pages I look,
Although the pages are dirty, wrinkled and worn.

How Jesus was born in Bethlehem,
Mary and Joseph laid baby Jesus on the hay.
Angels came, singing praises unto Him.
There wasn't any room at the Inn to stay.

Was a lowly stable, where the cattle were kept,
Where Our Saviour was born that holy night.
God must have smiled, maybe a tear of joy was wept,
For Jesus was born to give new life.

CHRISTMAS

C-----Is for CHRIST JESUS, born long ago.

H-----Is for HEAVEN from which He came.

R-----Is for the ROAD to Bethlehem.

I-----Is for No Room for them in the Inn.

S-----Is for the STAR that led the Wise Men.

T-----Is for TRUE LOVE He has for us.

M-----Is for the MANGER where Jesus was laid.

A-----Is for God's AMAZING grace.

S-----Is for our SAVIOR, who came to save.

New Year's Prayers

Dear Jesus, today is the beginning of a new year,
I pray You will draw me closer and closer, hear?
As each month, week and day goes by,
Your word in my heart I will hide.

To obey You in all things is my heart's desire,
Making me more like You, that others may see,
Not me, but only You, dear Jesus,
Now and forever, living in me.

I pray Your Holy Spirit,
Will fill me to overflow.
And spill out to others,
The love of Jesus shows.

Your healing power flows through me,
To others, who come my way.
You speak through me, Jesus,
The words You would have me say.

Only You, dear Jesus, let them see,
Hide me in Your shadow is my heart's plea.

Sunset Over Peace River And The Bay

While watching the sunset over Peace River and the bay,
I saw a beautiful scene at the close of the day.
God has turned the white clouds to pink and red,
As the golden sun begins to sink into its nightly bed.

Standing on the bridge, the ripple of water below,
God's beautiful sunset, shining all aglow.
A big pelican or two may fly by,
Looking for a place to rest for the night.

The reflection of color, dancing on the waves,
As though the sun was sinking into a watery grave.
It will shine tonight on other parts of the world,
As around the Earth it slowly whirls.

If God so chooses for us another day,
It will set again tomorrow over Peace River and the bay.
The waves will calm, as evening shadows again creep in,
The shining of the moon and stars will now begin.

The palms swaying in the evening breeze,
Rustling of the branches high in the trees.
Blue sky overhead with star twinkling lights,
What a beautiful time for Jesus to come tonight.

Punta Garda, Florida

Giving Thanks For A Beautiful Church

Some forty years ago, there was a vacant piece of land,
Thanks to God, today a beautiful church, now stands.
With it's white steeple, reaching upward to the sky,
As a token of God's love, for all to see as they go by.

Thank you Father, for a house of prayer,
Where You meet with us, anytime of day or hour.
Doesn't matter, if there is only one or two of us,
Jesus loves us so much, and in Him we must put our trust.

Here many have given their hearts to God,
Now the road to Heaven, they daily trod.
In the beautiful home, in Heaven so fair,
Those loved ones gone on before wait for us there.

As the years have come and gone,
We have worshipped God, in many a song.
Then from the pages of God's Holy Word,
Many messages about Jesus, have been heard.

The choir joins their voices together and sing
Praises to Jesus our Savior, Lord and King.
Pastor, Tommy Crawford, would preach God's word.
The Holy Spirit, drawing souls to Jesus, as they heard.

71

With the shouts of God's people, giving Him praise,
Hands lifted toward Heaven, with voices raised.
Thanking God, for loved ones saved from sin,
As they opened their heart's door asking Jesus in.

Loved ones and friends, from our church family are missed,
As you look about today, you could make a list.
They are singing praises to God, on the Heavenly shore,
Soon we shall join them, and fellowship together, forever more.

While working with Sammy, and the primary girls and boys,
What a blessing it was, and oh' what a joy.
As she stood by the door, Kleenex in her hand,
Out came the chewing gum, with a loving command.

She hugged each child, showing them God's love,
Today, she is home with Jesus, in Heaven above.
Tommy has joined her, and with the angles they sing,
Glory hallelujah, to Jesus our Savior, Lord and King.

On Easter morning as the sun peeped over the hill,
We gathered in Oak Hill Cemetery, sometimes a little chill.
As we began to sing and worship, Jesus our Lord,
All hearts were filled with praise, in one accord.

Our Savior, came forth from the grave long, long ago,
Please, Jesus, help us Your love, to others show.
May a likeness of You always show on our face,
For You died and arose for every color and race.

Those times, while kneeling at the altar in prayer,
Broken hearts, were shared with Jesus there.
Lots of answers came, while others still wait,
Some may not be answered, until we are inside Heaven's gate.

While gathered on Sunday nights, in B. Y. P. U.,
Taking a part, hoping to please my Jesus, too.
It helped me to read and study God's word,
Praying the message of Jesus would be heard.

Have you given your life to Jesus, trusting His love?
He will forgive your sins, give you a home above.
Fall on your knees, before Him today,
He know's your thoughts, hears every word you say.

Fort Robinson Church, holds many happy memories for me.
While we worshipped our Savior, others from sin, set free.
God's Holy Spirit. Will always fill this place,
As He continues to show His love and amazing grace.

As the church grows from year to year,
The broken hearts He knows, and He sees each tear.
Jesus will continue to heal, and save each heart,
If we trust Him, believing is our part.

I love everyone have missed the Church, through the years.
We'll meet again in Heaven, no more heartaches, pain or tears;
We will join altogether, giving God praise,
For Fort Robinson Church, friends, and memories of happy days.

We are so sorry, we can't be there to visit, and celebrate
On the Church's forty-fifth anniversary date.
We have a grandson, graduating from high school on this day,
Would you remember him in your prayers when you pray?
                    Love and prayers,
                    Velma
                    May 25, 1993

Written in answer to a letter from the church to celebrate
with them their forty-fifth anniversary of the church as
a charter member.

                              Fort Robinson Baptist Church
                              2012 Fort Robinson Drive
                              Kingsport, Tennessee

Days Of The Church Bell

Do you recall the days of the old church bells?
The memories and the stories they did tell,
As they rang out the good news from their steeples,
For God so loved all of the people.

On Sunday morning, a reminder of Sunday school,
Where parents and children gathered, was the rule.
To study God's word and to pray,
For loved ones lost or fallen by the way.

You could hear the bells ring out over the hills,
And the valleys too, what a thrill.
It was time for God's people to meet,
To lay their burdens at Jesus' feet.

The little country churches, painted so white,
With bells hanging in their steeples high.
There Jesus met with his people, back then.
Saved their souls from all of their sins.

Filled them with His spirit, to overflow,
The love of Jesus on their faces, did show.
People not ashamed to lift their hands in praise,
Singing glory hallelujah, with voices raised.

Those same bells told a different story,
Of loved ones who had gone home to glory.
Each ring would mean years in age,
Of life lived here on Earth and happy days.

And other bells, I love to hear them ring,
Were the old school Bells, how they did sing.
They no longer ring out for us,
They have taken them away, someplace to rust.

The Liberty Bell no longer chimes,
Its liberty is gone, also your and mine.
We still have it, but only by name,
Our liberty is gone, never to have again.

Little Salvation Army bells ring at Christmas time,
Gathering pennies, dollars, nickels and dimes.
For families without homes, food, anything to eat,
Children without toys, clothes, no shoes on their feet.

Christmas bells mean love, the love of God,
Jesus was born that day and a rough road He trod.
He gave His life on Mount Calvary,
He bled and died, for you and me.

The time once told by bells will be no more,
They will ring forever, on the other shore.
Jesus our Savior will be the light,
There will never, no never, be anymore night.

It's time to come home, my dear child,
You will hear those bells ring for miles and miles.
Throughout the heavens, their music will sound,
Glory hallelujah, we are homeward bound.

Who Do You Trust?

God said in His word, put your trust in no man.
Their deeds are evil, like sinking sand.
He saves and will help, through troubles and strife.
Put your trust only in Jesus, as you go through life.

Thinking Of A Dear Friend, Mary

It's four-thirty in the morning,
It's been another restless night.
I guess you, too, are awake,
Waiting the dawn of another day's light.

My mind goes back to our visit,
Only a week before God called him away.
The things we talked over and shared,
Not dreaming how near the day.

Dear friend, my heart goes out to you,
Tonight and in days to come.
May God give you great comfort,
After He has taken your loved one home.

May God enfold you in His arms,
Letting you know there is no harm.
He is there with you both day and night,
To keep you safe and to make decisions right.

Our heavenly Father does know all,
We must answer whatever the call.
He is always there, His love His power,
To comfort and help, whatever the hour.

You have been a blessing to me,
Not only you but others, you see.
I'm so sorry I can't be near,
Heartaches to help you bear.

Yes, God knows all, He sees each tear,
His ears, are open ready to hear.
Each prayer you pray, whatever the time,
Morning or night, through the coming years.

Who knows us better than Jesus, my dear?
Whatever the need, He is always near.
We must in faith believe His words of cheer,
With open hearts and ears to always hear.

Jeremiah 6:16 & 17

*Thus sayeth the Lord, Stand ye in the ways, and see,
and ask for the old paths, where is the good ways, and
walk therein, and ye shall find rest for your soul.*

*Also I set watchmen over you, saying, Hearken to the
sound of the trumpet.*

Isaiah 26:3 & 4

*Thou wilt keep him in perfect peace, whose mind is stayed
on Thee: because he trusteth in Thee*

*Trust ye in the Lord forever: for in the Lord Jehovah is
everlasting strength.*

Isaiah 41:10 –

Fear thou not: for I am with thee: be not dismayed: for I am thy God: I will strengthen thee: Yea, I will help thee: yea, I will uphold thee with the right hand of my righteousness.

Isaiah 42:9 & 10 –

Behold, the former things are come to pass, and new things do I declare: before they spring forth I tell you of them.

Sing unto the Lord a new song, and his praise from the end of the earth, ye that go down to the sea, and all that is therein: the isles, and the inhabitants thereof.

Isaiah 54:5 –

For the Maker is thine husband; the Lord of host is his name and thy Redeemer the Holy One of Israel; The God of the whole earth shall he be called.

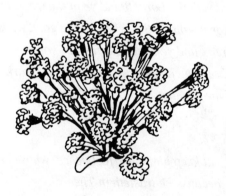

Come Home

I can feel the touch of God's hand on mine,
Saying, "Come home my child, everything is fine.
I will watch over your children, for you there,
And will save their souls, you have no fear."

But Jesus, what will my husband do?
Will You love him, and draw him closer too?
Your love for him, let it take my place,
Will You remind him of Your amazing grace?

Jesus, thank You for Your gentle love,
For giving me a home in Heaven above.
Jesus, I think of the lonely feeling,
While alone in the garden, You were kneeling.

I've lost my mother, daddy, sister, and my brother,
Your love is so precious, there is no other,
Who can take Your place, filling in the lonely hours?
While all alone I can feel Your power.

You erase each heartache and give me peace,
I'm going home to Heaven and rest at ease.
God Himself will fulfill His word,
Saving our loved ones who have never heard.

Yes, I can see those nail-scared hands,
They were nailed to the cross, just like God planned.
I can see the thorns upon your head,
Where the blood ran down your face, you shed.

Jesus, gave His life for you and me,
God must have cried when His Son He did see.
Hanging on the cross between Heaven and Earth,
Yes, God gave His Son, Jesus, to give us new birth.

Could you give up your child whom you love so?
To be crucified on a cross, I say no.
Do you love them enough to take their place?
Jesus, did for us, every nation and race.

Jesus, help me to love some soul for You today,
Hear You say, "Well done, my child," someday.
"You have fought a good fight, you've finished the race."
Will He be pleased with my life when I see His face?

Father help me to understand Your word,
Hiding it in my heart for some haven't heard.
That with Your help, show them the way,
To Jesus our Saviour forever be saved.

Father, put Your arms around my husband and children,
Love them for the rest of their days while living.
When their lives are finished down here,
Please, bring them all to Heaven to live with me there.

Our Loved Ones Are Going Home

The going home of our loved ones is never easy,
We must be thankful, for it's Jesus, that it pleases.
It makes Heaven more brighter each day,
It will draw us closer to Jesus, each step of the way.

Heaven will be brighter, because of one more mother,
For you and me, there will never be another.
On this Earth here, to go visit and see,
But in Heaven someday, we all shall be.

We must try to be happy, regardless the empty space,
Thinking of the smiles upon our Mother's face.
She is now with Jesus and loved ones too,
I'm getting anxious to go, what about you?

But Jesus said, "Wait, it is much too soon,
You still have work to do, while it's still noon."
The night shadows, will soon be creeping in,
Think of all those who are still out in sin.

Your life here you must still complete,
Reading God's word and pray, it may cost some sleep.
Our salvation to Jesus didn't come cheap.
As up Calvary's Mountain, He climbed so steep.

My child I love you, but Jesus said, "Come,
You have run your race, your work is done."
Now you must continue, singing God's praise,
With your hands toward Heaven and voices raised.

There are people who will listen to your songs,
That are still out in sin, doing wrong.
God will convict them of their sins,
They will open their heart's door, asking Jesus in.

So please don't weep for me, put a smile on your face,
Others, too, suffer heartaches of each color and race.
I will be waiting for you just inside the gate,
Carry your head up high, regardless the fate.

Time will go by faster, than you really know,
As the love of Jesus to others you show.
I know you will miss me, I'll miss you, too,
But God's work is important, and that you must do.

Now as I close my eyes and God takes my hand,
I'm going home to Jesus in Heaven's fair land.
Always take good care of your family here,
Because the coming of Jesus is Oh, so near.

Just call upon Jesus, at night or throughout the day,
He is always near and hears what you say.
Put your trust in Him, when loneliness creeps in,
Asking Him to fill each vacancy in your life then.

You will be so surprised, when you fully trust,
Believing in Jesus, you really must.
For each heartache and tear that you shed,
He will wipe away, for in His word He has said.

Taking each heartaches to Jesus and leaving them there,
Burdens, He will lift and answer prayer.
So lift your voice toward Heaven and sing,
Glory hallelujah, to our Lord, Saviour and King.

There is singing and shouting in Heaven today,
It won't be long, until we will hear what they say.
We will lift our voice and join right in,
We will be home with Jesus, Mother, family and friends.

"I love you Jesus"

Written in loving memory of:

My Aunt Roxie Lawson,
Mother of Mildred Lawson Courtney
and Mack Lewis (Buddy) Lawson

by Velma Brookshire

Homesick For Heaven

Dear Jesus, I'm homesick for Heaven tonight,
Waiting for Your coming in sight.
Then my soul will take its flight,
There will never be any more lonely nights.

Yes, Jesus I love You, tonight,
I need Your arms to hold me tight.
To feel Your very presence near,
Your still small voice, I long to hear.

Saying, come home with me today,
Heaven awaits with loved ones to stay.
Where angels are singing, streets are of gold,
Forgetting this world and the heartaches it holds.

There Jesus will wipe all tears away,
Forgetting how many I've shed along the way.
There will be peace and joy beyond compare,
Jesus, family and friends await me there.

I can almost see the lights of home,
The family waits for me around the throne.
Letting the glory hallelujah ring,
As they sing praises to our Lord and King.

Going Home

Shadows of death are in the making,
I can feel them creeping in.
But thanks to Jesus, for the taking,
My soul to heaven then.

I can hear the angels singing,
Giving praises to our king.
The joy bells are ringing,
Saying, "Come home, my redeemed."

I want to see my Jesus first of all,
The one who died on Calvary.
He shed His precious blood upon the tree,
While hanging there, for you and me.

On, how I love Him, Saviour and friend,
He forgave me of my sins,
Gave me joy and peace within,
Someday eternity with Him I will spend.

I can still hear my mother praying,
"Take care of my children, please."
Jesus, the same prayer I am saying,
Then I can sleep in peace and ease.

The family awaits me over yonder,
Other loved ones await me, too.
So farewell to this world of ponder,
On that bright shore, I'll wait for you.

Sitting Around My Father's Table

I can hear my Father say, "Come home, it's supper time."
I am making things ready, for my children to come and dine.
We will fellowship together, for all will be able
To give my Father thanks, as we sit around His table.

Jesus will be the one who will girt Himself and serve us,
Because in Him, we have fully put our trust.
What a glorious time that will be in Heaven so fair,
Sitting around my Father's table, worshipping Him there.

He will break the bread, just like He did long, long ago,
For the twelve disciples, because He loved them so.
He died to show His Love, when He hung upon the tree,
Around my Father's table, He has made a place for me.

Have you ever wondered, just what we will have to eat?
Really doesn't matter, the Bible says, "We will have a feast."
The cost of the meal, to us will never, never be payable,
Jesus paid the bill, "Come sit at my Father's table."

Can you imagine the millions who will be there?
Angels will be singing, God's heavenly hosts everywhere.
What a happy time of rejoicing, I cannot comprehend,
Feasting with the saints, around my Father's table then.

I can hardly wait to see my Savior's glorious face,
Knowing He died for all, regardless the color or race.
Have you given your heart to Jesus, dear friend and neighbor?
For soon we shall be, sitting around my Father's table.

The blessings of Heaven, showered on all who are there,
The light will be Jesus, shining everywhere.
We won't need a chandelier, to give us light,
Sitting around my Father's table, Jesus will shine bright.

Give your heart to Jesus, for you He still pleads,
Why wait any longer? He is all you really need.
You must get ready, while there is still time,
Then at my Father's table, you will with us dine.

I pray there won't be any empty chairs,
No troubles, heartaches, pain and no more tears.
Oh, how sad it will be for the circle to be broken,
Sitting around my Father's table, is only a small love token.

I'm getting anxious to see my Jesus, family and friends,
As we fellowship together, knowing time will never end.
Not even wondering, who will sit on my left and right,
My Father's table is ready, waiting for the Church, His bride.

There will be so much lost, if Heaven you miss,
Your soul will go to Hell, other things the Bible does list.
So my dear friends, think it over, before it's too late,
My Father's table is set and waiting, just inside Heaven's gates.

Evening Shadows

When evening shadows around me fall,
I once again listen for Jesus to call.
Although I watch and wait throughout the day,
There is something different, when at night I pray.

In the stillness of the midnight hours,
I can feel my Savior's love and power.
His still small voice is Oh, so sweet,
How I long to kneel at His dear feet.

When all others are sound asleep,
While reading God's word, I sometimes weep.
Praying for family and loved ones out in sin,
Wondering when will they ask Jesus in?

Time is so short, while here on Earth we live,
Why take a chance? Ask Jesus to forgive.
Then invite Him into your heart to stay.
You must go through Jesus, there is no other way.

Oh, the difference, Jesus will make in your life,
He will help through heartaches, trouble and strife.
When heartaches and troubles come your way,
He is there at all times, forever to stay.

How I long to go to my heavenly home above,
No sickness or pain, all will be joy, peace and love.
Jesus will wipe the tears from my eyes,
He has always heard me when I cried.

The Bible tells of mansions up there,
Streets of gold, beauty beyond compare.
Don't you want to go there? Jesus paid the cost,
For your soul and mine, which was lost.

As He hung there upon the cross that day,
I can almost hear my Savior say.
"Father, forgive them, they know not what they do."
In my mind I can see Him, what about you?

Oh, how I long to look upon His face,
Where the blood ran down, for the human race.
He took our place on Mount Calvary,
Bled and died, that we might go free.

The darkness that fell upon Jesus that day,
While He hung on the cross, our debt to pay.
God the Father, that moment turned His back,
Because the sins of the world are Oh, so black.

Could you give a daughter or a son,
To die on a cross? I say no, not one.
Yet God loves us so much, He gave Heaven's best.
For us a home in Heaven, when we are laid to rest.

Evening shadows are getting darker each night,
I will soon cross over to Heaven so bright.
Where never another pain, tear or heartache to be,
There Jesus, family and loved ones wait for me.

So, when Shadows are dark, just open God's word,
Listen Quietly, His voice can be heard.
Saying, "Cast all of your cares upon Me,
Time is passing fast, My face you soon shall see."

They say the darkest hours are just before dawn,
I'm waiting, wondering, dear Jesus, just how long
Will it be before You come for me?
Taking me home to Heaven, forever to stay.

Family and loved ones await me there,
Those left here behind, I leave in Your care.
Please save each one before it's too late,
I will wait for them, just inside Heaven's gates.

Don't weep for me, yourself you should cry,
If you don't know Jesus, I'm asking you, why?
So fall on your knees before Him today,
Asking Jesus into your heart, forever to stay.

Join me in Heaven, when your life here is over,
We will praise God together, forever more.
Thanking Him for Jesus, who paid the cost,
For us a home in Heaven, and not forever lost.

No more evening shadows, we will see,
Jesus is the light, shining for you and me.
His glory and brightness, eternally will shine,
Because there is no night, never no end of time.

Homecoming Day

The word Homecoming, has a beautiful sound –
Gathering of family, friends, loved ones all around.
With handshakes, smiles, a hug or a kiss.
Yes, there will be some whom we will miss.

Some have gone to that "Great Homecoming" above,
Gathered there with Jesus, family and friends they love.
Singing praises, while sitting at Jesus' feet,
Waiting for us and that "Great Heavenly Feast."

As we gather here, remembering yesterdays,
We must lift our voices and give Jesus praise.
Thanking Him for all He has done for us.
Saving our souls, while in Him we trust.

As we pray for each other, pastor will preach God's word.
There might be some who have never heard,
God loves us so much, He gave Jesus to die,
Upon the old rugged cross for you and I.

We greet our friends, haven't seen in a while,
Little ones are grown now, no longer a child,
Young adults married have children of their own,
Moved out of the community into their new homes.

Remembering back now, I was very small,
At the old revival meeting, when Jesus did call.
Knocking at my heart's door, waiting to come in,
To save my soul and to forgive me of my sin.

At that young age, I gave Jesus my heart,
Peace, joy and happiness, that moment did start.
He filled me with His Holy Spirit and His love.
I'm longing now for that Great Homecoming Above.

Those memories are still fresh in my mind to stay,
Each time I go back on Homecoming Day.
I want to say "Thank You, Jesus," once again,
As we lift our voices toward Heaven to sing.

People still come from miles all around,
Throughout the country and from small towns.
To greet their friends and loved ones, eat a good dinner,
Good cooks, you bet, they are all prize winners.

Menu! Fried chicken, turkey, ham, roast beef, good stew,
Meat loaf, soup beans, butter beans, potatoes, cole slaw, too,
Salads of all kinds, I could never name all,
You eat until you feel too full to crawl.

Sliced tomatoes, cucumbers, casserole of squash,
Green beans, baked beans, cream corn, I almost forgot.
Corn on the cob, sweet potatoes with nuts, marshmallows on top.
The list goes on and on, no place to stop.

There is coffee, Coca-Cola, Pepsi, Sprite, iced tea to drink.
Sugar and cream, just anything you want, I think.
Corn bread with butter, rolls, sliced bread, too.
Chocolate pie, pumpkin, lemon, custard, apple, to name a few.

You will find stack cake, chocolate, yellow and pound
Oblong in pans and dishes, some high and round.
Jello, desserts of many colors and kinds,
Oh yes, banana pudding, you keep in mind.

By the time you have gotten to the end of the line,
Not enough room on your plate for one thin dime.
You eat and eat, if still hungry, you can return,
Once again to the table, it's still with food overrun.

There are always lots of good things to eat,
Because Jesus has blessed and given us a feast.
For the good food, families, friends throughout our day.
So again, let us give Him thanks and praise.

We gather once again, for testimony and song,
Enjoying each one, doesn't matter how long.
It's joy to the soul, while giving God praise,
Singing, "When we all get to Heaven," with voices raised.

After all is over, ready for saying good-byes,
Sometimes little teardrops, will fill the eyes.
Knowing next Homecoming Day, some will be gone
Home to be with Jesus and friends, before too long.

So as we go our separate ways, traveling along,
Thinking of friends and loved ones and singing a song.
Someday, in Heaven a great table will be spread,
We will sit down with Jesus, He will break bread.

Oh, what a great Homecoming Day, that will be,
Jesus, family, friends and loved ones, we will see.
What peace and joy, we will have in our hearts,
Just knowing, never, never again we will have to part.

Our Days Are Coming To A Close

Tonight, as I think of God my Father, wondering how much longer He is giving me to live upon this wicked Earth. My heart goes out to my children, grandchildren and great, great grand-children, and people of all the world.

Father, I pray, please send your Holy Spirit of conviction to their hearts. Please, dear Father, in the name of Jesus, Your precious Son and my Saviour do save each soul.

God will give grace to all,
Who will truly believe in Him.

Asleep In Jesus

Two more of my dear friends,
You have recently taken home,
While sleeping peacefully in the night.
They are now with you, around God's throne.

Oh, the loneliness the family feels,
The empty space they leave behind.
Only Your presence and comfort
Can heal a broken heart and mind.

Searching For Jesus

Dear Jesus, where are you?
I have searched for you all day.
I need someone to talk to
And to listen when I pray.

Someone to tell my troubles to,
With an understanding love.
I need to feel Your spirit,
Coming down from Heaven above.

You have always been near me,
When I cry out to you in the night.
Oh, just to feel your presence
And your arms to hold me tight.

Satan keeps me so discouraged,
The battle seems to get worse by the day.
Please! Come quickly, dear Jesus,
Taking all my troubles and heartaches away.

The greatest peace I've ever known
Has always come from You –
Salvation, contentment and joy,
You have given the long nights through.

With all of my heart and mind I seek You.
Increase my faith and make me strong,
That I might be of help to others.
Please, dear Jesus, never let me go wrong.

Tonight, as I've searched for You,
As you reach down, taking me in Your arms,
Holding me tight through the long dark nights,
Assuring me of Your presence, keeping me from harm.

I need You every moment
Of my life; You let me live,
For without You, dear Jesus,
The loneliness no other can fill.

You are so sweet, loving and kind,
More like You I want to be,
With You in control of my life.
You in my life others will see.

Heather

Heather, I want to say, "Thank you, my dear."
For the beautiful artwork, you've done here.
You are truly blessed, with a gift from God,
Always use it for Him, as life's pathway you trod.

The tiny art, in the corners of each page,
May others behold, with a glimpse, maybe a gaze.
Reminding them for you always to pray,
To keep you before God in prayer, both night and day.

The name you carry means a flower,
I'm sure Mother and Dad knew, in that hour,
You were born a special gift to them,
Your hands, were already blessed of Him.

The name "Heather" has a beautiful sound,
As a flower, it is known all around.
Your name, too, is known by Jesus above,
Just like the flower, God filled you with His love.

Again, I want to thank you, for the art,
You will always hold a special spot in my heart.
Still not knowing what I will do with my writtings,
Praying someday in other hearts they will be hiding.

Life's Finished Task

The time has come; now I must say
Good-bye to all of you,
To family and friends and some I've only know
For just a day or two.

If I've said or done anything to hurt you,
Would you please forgive me, I pray?
My life has been an open book
And read by God each day.

Jesus forgave me of my sins
From beginning through the end.
He covered each page with His blood,
It was in Him my faith began.

My life by no means has been perfect,
I'm only a small piece of clay.
I pray I might have been a tiny blessing
To someone who has passed my way.

There have been heartaches and failures,
Jesus picked me up when I would fall.
Through the years I've really tried
To live for Him through them all.

Some of you who read this or maybe listen
To others, you may have caused heartaches and pain.
Did you ask them to forgive you?
And God to fill you heart with love after the shame?

Have you wondered what Jesus will say
When you meet Him at Heaven's door?
Will He say, "Welcome home, my child"?
Or turn you away to Hell forever more?

I'm going home to meet my Jesus,
See my family, loved ones and friends.
The only sadness I find within my heart
Is for those still lost out in sin.

To my family and friends, all I can leave you
Is God's word, my love and prayers.
I ask that you search the depths of your soul,
Give your all to Jesus, He died because He cares.

I have passed down the road, you now follow,
Taking Jesus by the hand.
Yes, I've gone now, it will be lonely.
But, I'll wait for you in that happy land.

Please, take care of all the children,
Teach them of Jesus and you lead the way.
I pray the family circle won't be broken,
We will all be home in Heaven, some sweet day.

My life is a finished task,
God closed the last chapter just the other day.
Would you please bow your heads and pray?
Jesus will come into your heart, believing when you ask.

As you close the covers of this book,
Of all the contents you have looked –
Did you receive a blessing of some kind
For you heart, soul or mind?

The words God has given, put into rhyme
Since 1990, from time to time,
In my heart I'm still amazed
To God in Heaven goes all the praise

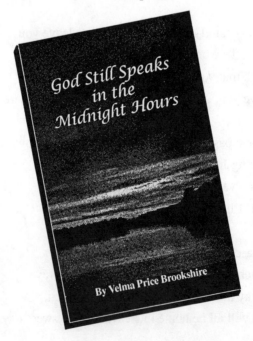

God Still Speaks
in the
Midnight Hours

By Velma Price Brookshire

I sincerely thank you with all my heart,
For sharing some of your time with me.
All my love and prayers

Velma Price Brookshire

Velma Price Brookshire